Bicycles

Chris Oxlade

H www.heinemann.co.uk
Visit our website to find out more information about Heinemann Library books.

To order:
☎ Phone 44 (0) 1865 888066
▤ Send a fax to 44 (0) 1865 314091
▢ Visit the Heinemann Bookshop at www.heinemann.co.uk to browse our catalogue and order online.

First published in Great Britain by Heinemann Library, Halley Court, Jordan Hill, Oxford OX2 8EJ a division of Reed Educational and Professional Publishing Ltd.
Heinemann is a registered trademark of Reed Educational & Professional Publishing Ltd.

OXFORD MELBOURNE AUCKLAND
JOHANNESBURG BLANTYRE GABORONE
IBADAN PORTSMOUTH (NH) USA CHICAGO

Designed by Paul Davies and Associates
Originated by Ambassador Litho Ltd
Printed in Hong Kong/China

04 03 02 01
10 9 8 7 6 5 4 3 2

ISBN 0 431 10840 4

British Library Cataloguing in Publication Data

Oxlade, Chris
  Bicycles. – (Transport around the world)
  1.Bicycles – Juvenile literature
  I.Title
  629.2'22

Acknowledgements
The Publishers would like to thank the following for permission to reproduce photographs: Allsport: Frank Baron p16, David Cannon p17; Corbis: Karl Weatherly p6, Hulton-Deutsch Collection pp8, 9, Bettmann p10, Phil Schermeister p20, Galen Rowell p22, Peter Turnley p24, Earl Kowall p25; Stockfile: pp7, 15; The Stock Market: Paul Barton p4, Charles Gupton p5; Tony Stone Images: Hulton Getty p10, Chris Shinn p12, Lori Adamski Peek p13, Greg Adams p14, Jean-Marc Truchet p28; Trip: J Ringland pp18, 19, S Grant p23, T Freeman p26, G Contorakes p27, G Howe p29

Cover photograph reproduced with permission of Tony Stone

Every effort has been made to contact copyright holders of any material reproduced in this book. Any omissions will be rectified in subsequent printings if notice is given to the Publisher.

Contents

Any words appearing in the text in bold, **like this**, are explained in the glossary.

What is a bicycle?

A bicycle is a machine that moves along on two wheels. Many people use bicycles to go to work or school or just for fun. The rider sits on a seat called a saddle and **pedals** along.

Balancing on a bicycle can be tricky at first. This child's bike has small extra wheels called stabilisers. They stop the bicycle falling over.

How bicycles work

The rider makes a bicycle move along by turning the **pedals** with his or her feet. The pedals pull on the **chain** and the chain makes the back wheel go round.

Brakes make the bicycle slow down. To work the brakes the rider pulls a **lever** on the handlebar. This makes **rubber** blocks press against the wheel.

First bicycles

The first bicycles were called hobbyhorses.
They did not have **pedals**. Instead the rider
moved the hobbyhorse along by pushing
his or her feet against the ground.

These bicycles were made about 100 years ago. They have pedals and **chains** like modern bicycles, and **rubber** tyres on their wheels.

Penny-farthing

This strange bicycle is called a penny-farthing. It was first made in about 1870. Its name comes from the names of two old British coins.

The **pedals** of a penny-farthing are on the huge front wheel. The rider sits on a saddle above the wheel. Getting on and off is very tricky.

Where are bicycles used?

Many people ride their bicycles on roads. In China, millions of people travel to and from work on their bicycles. Not many people have cars.

Some bicycles can travel off the road on bumpy **dirt tracks** and paths. People use these kinds of bicycles to cycle into the countryside or up hills and mountains.

Mountain bikes

A mountain bike is a bicycle for riding over rough or muddy ground. The rider is wearing a helmet in case she falls off.

Tyres with a chunky **tread** stop the bike slipping on muddy ground. The **suspension** lets the wheels move up and down as the bicycle goes over bumps.

Racing bikes

Cyclists race against each other on roads or cycle tracks. They ride special racing cycles which can travel at more than 50 kilometres per hour.

Some racing cycles have solid **frames** and wheels. These let the cycle go faster through the air. The rider wears a special smooth helmet.

frame

Trick bikes

Riders can perform many trick moves on trick bikes called BMX bikes. They ride from side to side along a **half-pipe**, doing spins and **somersaults**.

On a BMX bike, short rods stick out from the centre of each wheel. The rider stands on the rods to do spins, hops and **wheelies**.

rod

Recumbent bikes

This strange looking vehicle is a bicycle called a recumbent bicycle. The rider lies back in a seat instead of sitting up.

The **pedals** on a recumbent bicycle are at the front instead of in the middle. A long **chain** goes all the way to the back wheel.

Touring bikes

People who go on long journeys by bicycle use special touring bicycles. These bicycles are good for cycling on different sorts of ground, such as roads and rough tracks.

Touring bicycles have racks where you can store equipment such as tents. Bags called panniers can be fixed to the racks.

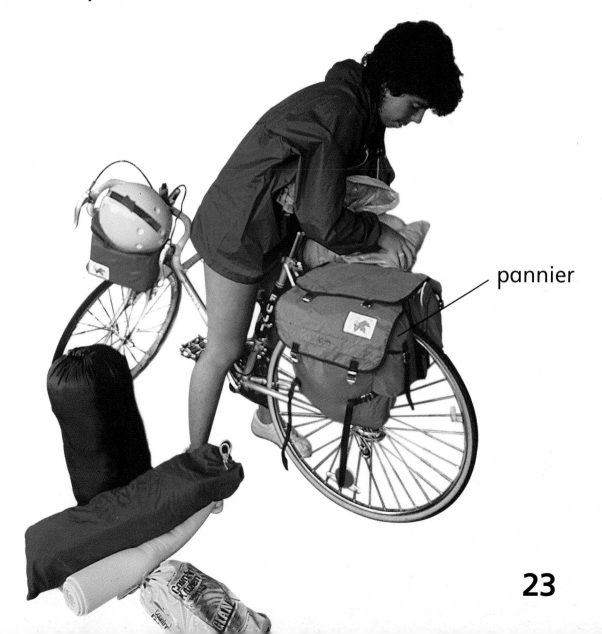

pannier

Rickshaws

A cycle rickshaw carries passengers in seats. The cyclist sits in front of the passengers. In some countries, like India, people hire rickshaws instead of taxis.

Some rickshaws have a hood over the seats in case of rain. They often have colourful pictures and decorations on the seats, hood and handlebars.

Tandems

A tandem is a bicycle for two people to ride. It has two saddles and two sets of handlebars. The person who sits at the front is in charge of **steering**.

A tandem also has two pairs of **pedals**, one for each rider. They are joined together by a **chain**. To keep going, both riders have to pedal at the same speed.

Unicycles

The letters 'uni' mean 'one'. So a unicycle has only one wheel. Riding a unicycle takes lots of practice. It's even trickier to carry on juggling!

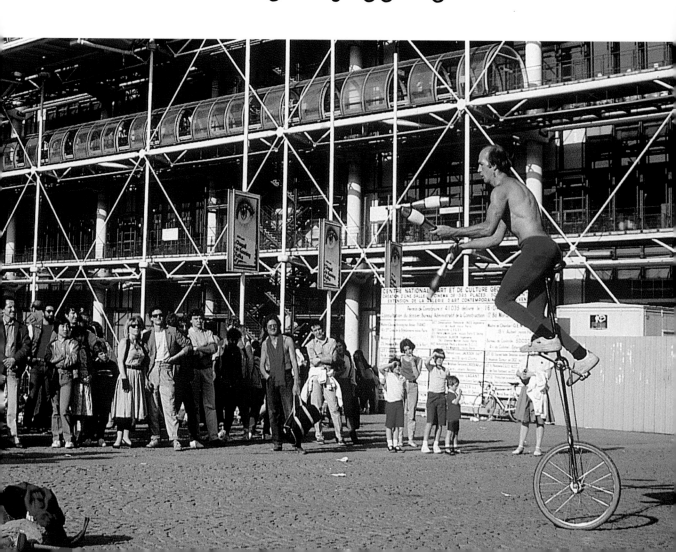

On a unicycle the rider can **pedal** backwards and forwards. The rider needs to keep pedalling to move along and to stay balanced.

Timeline

1700s The first type of bicycle is called a hobbyhorse. It has no **pedals** or brakes.

1861 The first bicycle with pedals is built. The pedals make the front wheels turn.

1870 The first penny-farthing bicycle appears. It has a huge front wheel and a tiny back wheel.

1874 A type of bicycle called a safety bicycle is invented. It has a **chain** and brakes, and looks like a modern bicycle.

1888 John Dunlop invents a bicycle tyre filled with air, called a pneumatic tyre. Before this, tyres were made with solid **rubber**.

1903 Cyclists set out on the first *Tour de France* cycle race. The race is about 4000 kilometres long and takes three weeks.

Glossary

chain   a loop made of metal pieces that joins a bicycle's pedals to its back wheel

dirt track   a narrow road with a surface of earth

frame   the main piece of a bicycle that all the other parts are attached to. Most frames are made of metal tubes joined together.

half-pipe   a special track for trick bicycles. It has round slopes on each side, like a tube cut in two.

lever   a bar

pedal   the part of the bicycle where the rider pushes with his or her feet to move the bicycle along

rubber   a soft, bendy material that is used to make tyres and brake blocks on bicycles

somersault   a trick move when a rider goes head over heels and lands back on the wheels

steering   guiding which way the bicycle is going

suspension   the part of the bicycle that joins the wheels to the rest of the bicycle

tread   the part of the tyre that touches the road

wheelie   a bicycle trick when a rider pedals along balanced on the back wheel with the front wheel in the air

Index